Formas: triángulos
Shapes: Triangles

Esther Sarfatti

Rourke
Publishing LLC

Vero Beach, Florida 32964

www.rourkepublishing.com

PHOTO CREDITS: © Marilyn Nieves: title page; © Stas Volik: page 5; © Nicholas Monu: page 7; © Stephen Walls: page 9; © Kenneth C. Zirkel: page 11; © Christine Balderas: page 13; © Viktor Kitaykin: page 15; © Joan Kimball: page 17; © Tristin Hurst: page 23.

Editor: Robert Stengard-Olliges

Cover design by Nicola Stratford.

Library of Congress Cataloging-in-Publication Data

Sarfatti, Esther.
  Shapes : triangles / Esther Sarfatti.
     p. cm. -- (Concepts)
  ISBN 978-1-60044-528-6 (Hardcover)
  ISBN 978-1-60044-669-6 (Softcover)
  1. Triangle--Juvenile literature. 2. Shapes--Juvenile literature. I. Title.
   QA482.S36 2008
   516'.154--dc22
                              2007014076

Printed in the USA

CG/CG

www.rourkepublishing.com – rourke@rourkepublishing.com
Post Office Box 3328, Vero Beach, FL 32964

Esto es un triángulo.
This is a triangle.

Hay triángulos por
todas partes.

Triangles are everywhere.

Este tejado tiene un triángulo.

This roof has a triangle.

Estos sándwiches son triángulos.

These sandwiches are triangles.

Estas ventanas son triángulos.

These windows are triangles.

Este barquillo de helado es un triángulo.

This ice cream cone is a triangle.

13

Algunas guitarras
son triángulos.

Some guitars are triangles.

15

Esta colcha tiene triángulos.

This quilt has triangles.

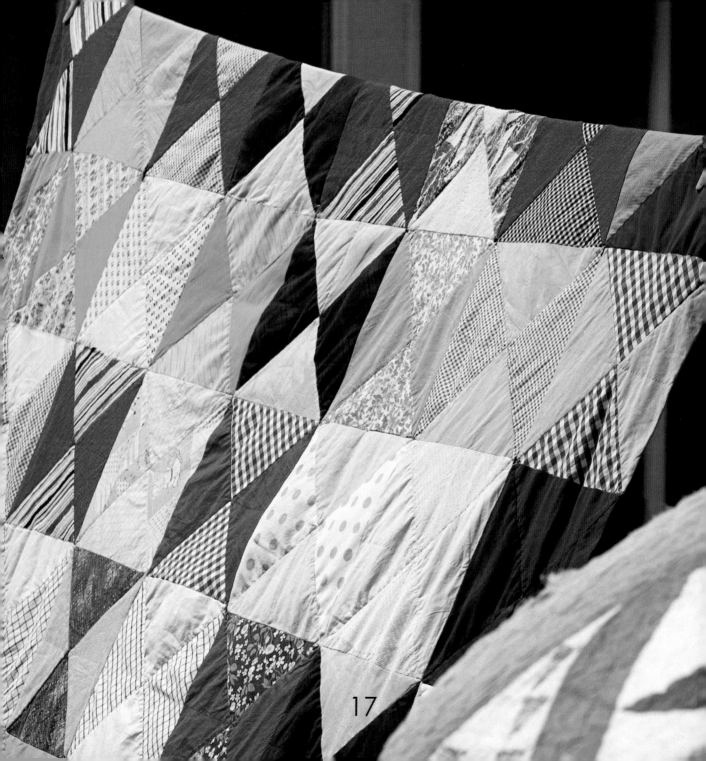

17

Este trozo de pastel es
un triángulo.

This piece of pie is
a triangle.

Este queso es un triángulo.

This cheese is a triangle.

21

Hay triángulos por
todas partes.
¿Puedes encontrar
los triángulos?

Triangles are everywhere.
Can you find the triangles?

23

Índice

Index

Lecturas adicionales / Further Reading

Leake, Diyan. *Finding Shapes: Triangles*. Heinemann, 2005.
Olson, Nathan. *Triangles Around Town*. A+ Books, 2007.

Páginas Web recomendadas / Recommended Websites

www.enchantedlearning.com/themes/shapes.shtml

Acerca de la autora / About the Author

Esther Sarfatti lleva más de 15 años trabajando con libros infantiles como editora y traductora. Ésta es su primera serie como autora. Nacida en Brooklyn, Nueva York, donde creció en una familia trilingüe, Esther vive actualmente en Madrid, España, con su esposo y su hijo.

Esther Sarfatti has worked with children's books for over 15 years as an editor and translator. This is her first series as an author. Born in Brooklyn, New York, and brought up in a trilingual home, Esther currently lives with her husband and son in Madrid, Spain.